ISBN: 978-1482650334

First Printing, 2015

Printed in the United States of America

Ukulele Mastery Simplified

How Anyone Can Quickly Become a Strumming, Chords and Melodic Uke Ninja

By: Erich Andreas

Liability Disclaimer

By reading this document, you assume all risks associated with using the advice given below, with a full understanding that you, solely, are responsible for anything that may occur as a result of putting this information into action in any way, and regardless of your interpretation of the advice.

You further agree that our company cannot be held responsible in any way for the success or failure of your business as a result of the information presented below. It is your responsibility to conduct your own due diligence regarding the safe and successful operation of your business if you intend to apply any of our information in any way to your business operations.

Terms of Use

You are given a non-transferable, "personal use" license to this product. You cannot distribute it or share it with other individuals.

Also, there are no resale rights or private label rights granted when purchasing this document. In other words, it's for your own personal use only.

Quick Summary

How to Use This Book: There are an infinite amount of pages that could be written on the subject of any musical instrument. With that being said, typically there are only a few fundamentals that we truly need to master in order to play an instrument.

With that thought in mind, this book will cover what you need to know to be a GREAT ukulele player. Don't be fooled by a 300 page book on how to play ukulele. I could write a 300 page book on how to play tic-tac-toe, but I can also show you within a couple of sentences how to play the game that would last you your entire life.

The ukulele is a simple instrument. It was designed to be, and its design is the very reason why it is a fairly easy instrument to master. Can you get complicated on the uke? Yes you can! And there are some great players that have brought it to a new level.

However, it still only has four strings and is a common, "folk" instrument. So let's not over think the process and let's have some fun! This book was written and designed so that you can quickly master the ukulele. It will allow you to play in any key and various genres of music.

The book was specifically designed to be read step by step. Each principle builds upon the next, so it's important to NOT skip around.

I know that there are some of you out there that want to go to a specific section and just jump right in. For those of you that have been playing for a while and want to do this, then feel free to. However, if you don't understand that specific chapter, you will most likely need to follow the book in order.

I've condensed this book into what I believe are the first and most important lessons that any and every ukulele player should master.

So, are you ready to do this thing? Let's go!

Introduction

Congratulations for finding this book and THANK YOU for purchasing it! By purchasing this book, as well as viewing my videos at www.youtube.com/yourukesage, I am allowed to reach people all around the world...and for that I am very grateful!

Before we begin, I want to let you know a little about myself and my approach towards teaching ukulele. I have been playing stringed instruments (guitar, ukulele, and bass) for over 25 years and have been in numerous bands (rock, metal, country, pop, alternative) during that time.

I have studied with many teachers and was a classical guitar major for 3 years before changing my major and graduating with a Music Business degree. I am a working studio guitar/ukulele/bass player as well as a guitar teacher, songwriter, producer and live performer.

I LOVE playing music as a "job" and I am *living my dream!* I also **LOVE** imparting others with knowledge so that they, too, can fulfill their dreams as it relates to music. I originally set out to teach music to a lot of people all over the world with a method that was fun, painless and to the point.

I have taught music on and off since I was about 17. First, I just taught my friends and eventually 100s of musicians professionally. I moved to Nashville, TN in 1990 and immediately hit the ground running. My clientele consists of students from ALL age groups and all walks of life including students, professionals, writers, producers, artists and record companies.

Since I have always been so obsessed with the music, teaching sometimes up to 65 students a week was not enough! SO, I started teaching for free on YouTube. My ukulele channel is located at www.youtube.com/yourukesage and my guitar channel is located at www.youtube.com/yourguitarsage. Last I checked in the winter of 2015, my YourGuitarSage YouTube channel at www.youtube.com/yourguitarsage had over 39 million views and over 175 thousand subscribers.

On that channel I have taught hundreds of songs and techniques in MANY genres of music. I have received literally thousands of letters/e-mails from folks in countries saying that they don't have the resources or money to take one-on-one lessons and that the only way they've learned how to play was through me, Erich Andreas.

SOOO...Thank you for allowing me to guide YOU in this great learning process. I am thankful for this great opportunity!

A word of encouragement - Some of the concepts that you are about to learn are quite "thick" with information; you *will* be challenged to do some serious thinking about the uke. Your hands will be as equally challenged. Many players can mimic other players, but often times they don't know the "whys" of what they are doing or even how to be creative themselves.

This guide will unravel much of that. Your fingers will be more challenged than ever before. Your mind will be stretched much further as well. There is a reason why babies drink mother's milk from birth, yet as they grow older, start eating solid food. This learning process is the same and it is crucial that you keep that in mind.

Before embarking on this journey, you must remember that you *will* get discouraged at times! You *will* get frustrated – and most likely, you will want your skills to progress faster...and to that I say, welcome to the club!

Most every musician wants things to move faster than they typically do. The greatest musicians have *all* felt these frustrations and have also felt, at times, that they were not "cut out" for music. BUT, like all good and worthy endeavors, we must strive for the mark.

If gold were just a few inches beneath the soil in our own backyard, we would be digging it up all day and probably wouldn't appreciate it much at all. But because it's found deeper – and requires considerable effort to extract– it's much more valuable and appreciated *that much more*!

So be encouraged!

Remember that the time you spend on your uke *will* pay off! Have *fun* and spend as much time as you can practicing and honing your skills. I promise you *will* see *great progress*!!

NOW DIG IN!

Chapter 1:

Discover the Anatomy of the Ukulele While Getting to Know Your Uke

The ukulele: The ukulele, or uke for short, is a four string guitar-like instrument that originated from Hawaii in the 19th century. The strings are typically made from nylon or "gut". The ukulele strings are traditionally plucked or strummed with the nails or fingertips of the strumming hand while the other hand "frets" the strings in order to change the pitches of the notes or chords. The sound resonates throughout the body of the ukulele and is emitted through the sound hole.

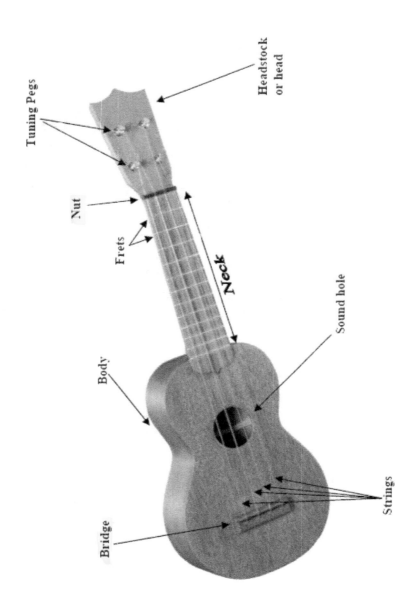

Tuning Pegs

Nut

Frets

Headstock or head

Neck

Sound hole

Body

Bridge

Strings

Chapter 2:

How to Choose a Ukulele for Purchase

Choosing a uke is an exciting, but sometimes confusing undertaking because of all the variables that you might feel are involved.

What brand is best?

What type of woods are best?

Should I get a ukulele with a "pickup" or not?

What style...size...color and then what about all the things you don't know about ukes, right?

Let's simplify the process a bit.

When directing a student to a new uke purchase, the main variables for me always come down to: *budget, feel* and *sound* (in no particular order). Trying a bunch of ukes in your price range will give you a great education on feel and sound. I KNOW you want the pretty red uke, but don't pick the uke because it's red if it sounds or plays poorly. The prettiness will get old. Poor sound or feel does not go away.

If you have a $50 budget, there is no need in seriously looking at the $400 ukes, although knowing what they feel and sound like would be helpful to your education. I have some expensive ukes and some "cheapos." Sometimes more money gets you "more uke" and sometimes more money just makes you think you are getting a better uke.

DON'T let the price alone dictate a uke purchase. You will be regretful. So, figure out what your budget is and try to stick to it. You can get an acceptable $100 uke if you know what to look for.

I have ukes priced from $20 to several hundred dollars, but none were purchased on price alone. Let me clarify: more expensive TYPICALLY equate to better, but be careful in using price alone to determine a ukes worth.

Feel is an important variable in choosing an instrument. There are four basic types of ukuleles:

Soprano: this is the most common type of ukulele and it is most recognizable by its very small body. The tuning is G, C, E, A.

Concert: this is also a common ukulele type and the type that you will see me play in my videos at:

www.youtube.com/yourukesage. Concert ukulele bodies are slightly bigger than soprano ukes. They are also tuned G, C, E, A.

Tenor: this ukulele is even bigger yet, being slightly larger than the concert ukulele. It has a slightly fuller tone and is also tuned G, C, E, A.

Baritone: this ukulele is the biggest of the four. It has the fullest sound and is tuned like the higher four strings of the guitar. That tuning is D, G, B, E.

In regards to which one you should purchase, I would suggest the concert ukulele. To me a baritone ukulele is a bit redundant to the guitar. Personally, if I want that sound I will pick up a classical guitar which has nylon strings like the ukulele.

The concert ukulele is small enough to be very portable and has that classic ukulele sound. However, that is just my suggestion. Ultimately it's your decision and you need to go with the instrument that moves you the most.

String action is also important as high action (string height) can make chording and fretting difficult and discouraging. The only way for you to know what is "normal" or "high" is, is to try a bunch of ukuleles. Try some expensive ones too, so you can get an idea for different price ranges and what the extra money may or may not buy you.

Okay, so all that said, make sure the "feel" of the ukulele is the best out of all the ukes that you try.

Sound is the other important variable.

Different woods and their ages, and ukulele construction, are some of the variables that dictate the sound of the uke. Make sure that you are comparing apples to apples, such as comparing ukes in the same room, playing the same songs, etc. This will assure that you have the same dynamics and acoustical environment. USE THE SAME VARIABLES!

Buying a first ukulele is best done at a store where you can get an education in the process. Don't be afraid to ask questions, try a bunch of ukes and get what you want! Be polite, but you are getting ready to spend some money, so don't be rushed or talked into something that does not resonate with you (feel, sound and budget). It's okay to consider other prices and find out about different woods, etc. but ultimately it's what YOU are most happy with, not the sales person.

Take brand names with a grain of salt. There is not a best ukulele, only what's best for you. That is, don't buy a ukulele just because of the name. I have brand name ukuleles that you would know

and others that you would not, but I love them all for different reasons.
BUDGET, FEEL and SOUND... repeat the mantra after me... BUDGET, FEEL and SOUND... BUDGET, FEEL and SOUND.

Now go fall in love with a uke!

Chapter 3:

How Proper Posture and Using Your Fingertips Will Dramatically Increase Your Playing Accuracy

The First Ukulele Lesson That I Teach EVERY New Student:

No matter the style of playing, <u>EVERY</u> student must understand a few basic principle techniques that they will use for the rest of their ukulele playing. THIS is the uke lesson that covers them!

I'm going to break this down into some basic bite-sized pieces:

Posture -Although sometimes used with a strap, the ukulele is traditionally tucked under the strumming arm while the strumming hand strums on the neck (Unlike traditional guitar strumming where the player traditionally strums directly over the sound hole). Check out my videos at:

http://www.youtube.com/user/yourukesage to see this in action.

This technique takes a little bit of practice but in short time will become more comfortable, making the ukulele playable at a moment's notice.

FINGERTIPS!!! This is **THE #1 rule for ALL beginner ukulele players**. For the fretting-hand, play on your fingertips! Playing on the "pads" of your fingers is bad practice and will make for sloppy playing and all sorts of frustration later down the road.

A good rule of thumb to remember is: ALWAYS keep the top knuckle of your fretting-hand curled: the more, the better as a hard, fast rule. The only exception to this is when you are playing bar chords. Bar chords require "barring" your finger across several strings at once in order to play a chord.

Chapter 4:

How to Read Ukulele Tablature – Part 1

Ukulele tablature is a system of notation that graphically represents music by showing you the strings and frets that are to be played. It also can show some degree of "feel" or technique with slides, hammer-ons, pull-offs, slurs, vibrato, etc.

Since tablature is somewhat of a shortcut system there are not a lot of official rules to this notation. In fact, transcriptions vary from tab to tab as one transcriber may illustrate an idea differently than another. I'm going to try to be as thorough as possible regarding the subject so that you have a good grasp of how to interpret it.

In tablature, a note is represented by placing a number (which indicates the fret to play), on the appropriate string. One thing that tablature does not illustrate is the duration of notes. It does not tell you how long a note should be held out. Sometimes tab transcribers will specifically put longer spaces between notes on the line to denote duration, but it's not quantifiable; it is simply a basic idea. Since most people don't use tablature unless it's a song that they already know and can hum, so this part becomes less of an issue, except maybe with more intricate parts.

<u>In tablature, each line represents a string on the uke</u>. The top string (in proximity to the ground) is the bottom line (see illustration below) and the bottom string (closest to the ground) is the top line. So basically, it's the opposite of the way that you think it might be. One way to remember this is to think of the **higher lines as the higher pitched strings and the lower lines as the lower pitched strings.**

1st string or A-----------------------------

2nd string or E-----------------------------

3rd string or C-----------------------------

4th string or G-----------------------------

The numbers placed on those lines represent the frets, NOT which finger is used. Tablature does NOT *typically* tell you what fingers to use. That is where a great instructor and/or proper technique come in handy!

When numbers are placed vertically as below,

you will play the notes simultaneously like a chord (all at once), as in a strum.

Below is a G major chord.

1st string or A------2---------------------

2nd string or E-----3---------------------

3rd string or C------2---------------------

4th string or G------0---------------------

Part 2 of this section can be found later in the book. For now, you will only need to understand the principles in Part 1.

Chapter 5:

Top 3 Strengthening Exercises That Will Sharpen Your Finger Speed and Technique

"Getting your fingers to do what you want them to do..."

According to Webster's dictionary, dexterity is, "the readiness and grace in physical activity; especially the skill and ease in using the hands". Well that obviously applies to us uke players; the more you do a particular exercise or movement, the better you become.

In fact, our brains are designed in such a way that it's impossible for you to not get better when you practice. That means that any amount of playing on the uke whatsoever is beneficial. Now when we practice specifically, deliberately and with repetition, we end up gaining a lot of control over our fingers - or anything else that we set our mind to, for that matter.

Since our thumb is located so closely to our first and second fingers, our third and fourth fingers don't get called on for the same amount of tasks throughout the day.

For this reason, <u>EVERYONE'S</u> third and fourth fingers tend to be lazy when playing the uke. You thought it was just you? Nope! Everyone's third and fourth fingers are lazy and need to be developed with such exercises. :)

The following three exercises were specifically designed to strengthen your fingers and hands, increase your speed and sharpen your technique. I have used these exercises for years and have found them to be extremely beneficial.

Exercise one is a warm-up just to get your fingers moving.

Exercise two is an intense workout that develops both left and right hands. You will especially feel the third and fourth finger of your fretting hand being worked out through this one. Make sure that you're using the appropriate finger on the appropriate fret throughout the exercise. For instance, when you start playing frets two and three, make sure you are using fingers two and three. When you're playing frets three and four, make sure you are playing with fingers three and four.

Exercise three is a unique exercise that will seriously challenge you and require you to play on your fingertips. Don't be concerned if you can't do this exercise right away. It's definitely one you want to work up to. This third exercise can be fingerpicked or sweep picked. If you are going to do the sweep pick, pick the first three notes down and the second three notes up. Also make sure that when you do pick each string, it's done in a sweeping motion - NOT picking each note individually. It should be a smooth motion, allowing the pick to do the work.

At the top of these dexterity exercises, you will see I also cover four things that you always want to remember when playing these exercises. Let me give you a little bit of theory as to why we are doing each of these things.

1. **Playing on your fingertips makes a uke player faster and more efficient.** The more you play on your fingertips the lighter your touch will be and the less hand fatigue you will experience. It's also very important to have control over what part of the finger you use. Since the fingertips seem to be the hardest part to master, learning this first will make everything else seem easier. Uke players that play on their fingertips tend to play chords cleanly. Uke

players that play on the pads of their fingers tend to play chords sloppily.

2. **Playing right behind the fret requires much less pressure than playing further back.** Think about the leverage of a seesaw. The position of the fulcrum "that part under the center of the seesaw that balances it" determines how much leverage you have. On a see-saw, if the fulcrum is in the correct place, a small child can easily lift a large man off the ground. Similarly, leveraging your finger closer to the fret will allow you to play more quickly and efficiently.

3. **Playing with all your fingers is very important because, as you become a more accomplished player, you will most likely be playing faster and/or more complex arrangements.** Running out of fingers is no fun! So be proactive and use that third and fourth finger. I have had many students over the years thank me for insisting that they use their third and fourth fingers.

4. **Lastly, it's helpful to leave some space between the palm of your fretting hand and the uke neck because it allows you to more easily play on your fingertips and ultimately have more control of your hand.** At first, this can be a little awkward. Most beginners grab the neck like a shovel and their thumb comes right over the neck. And that's perfect... if you are digging a hole with your uke! But you're not...so don't!

What we do on the uke requires a lot more finesse and a much different approach than digging a hole. If we have a uke strap holding up our uke or if our uke is properly tucked underneath our strumming arm, then it's not going anywhere. Once you are truly aware of this, it will liberate your hand from grappling the neck.

For new players, grappling the neck can really limit your playing. Later on in your playing you may be able to be more carefree, but for now try to stick to good technique.

I am often times asked, *"How long should I practice this exercise?"* To which, I pose this question, *"how good do you want to get?"*

Obviously, the more you practice these exercises, the better you'll become. If you want to become great, you should practice it a lot. If you are perfectly fine with mediocrity, then you don't have to play as much. Alright, enough talk! Off you go!!!

- Play directly on your fingertips - make sure your fingernails on your "fretting" hand are always trimmed.

- Play right behind the fret (this is for leverage). Remember the see-saw example.

- Play with ALL your fingers (each finger plays a specific fret)

- It is best to leave some space between the palm of your hand and the neck. This will give you much needed leverage to play on your fingertips. Curling the last knuckle on your finger(s) is also helpful.

Dexterity Exercise #1- The Foundation Builder

Dexterity exercise #1 is a GREAT exercise for beginners to advanced players. You can practice it for long periods of time and is great for general agility and strength.

```
1st string or A---1-2-3-4-------------------------------------
2nd string or E---------------1-2-3-4-------------------------
3rd string or C---------------------------1-2-3-4-------------
4th string or G---------------------------------------1-2-3-4---
```

Dexterity Exercise #2 – Mix It Up

Dexterity Exercise #2 is designed for intermediate to advanced players and is a great agility and strength builder. You will especially feel a "burn" when using fingers 3 and 4. This will quickly get your 3rd and 4th finger to be as nimble as fingers 1 and 2.

```
A---1-2---------------2-3-----------------3-4-------------

E------1-2----------1-2-----2-3----------2-3----3-4---------

C--------1-2-----1-2--------2-3-----2-3----------3-4-----

G------------1-2--------------- 2-3-----------------3-4 etc
```

Dexterity Exercise #3 – Get Crazy with It

Dexterity Exercise #3 is for ADVANCED players! It is a MAJOR strength builder and

35

perfect for building chordal dexterity, stretch (reach) and strength. Take your time moving into this exercise. It's very challenging!

```
A-----10---------10-------10-------10--------9------
E----9---9----9---9----9---9----8---8----8---8----
C---8-----8--8-----8--7-----7--7-----7--7------7--
G--7--------6--------6--------6--------6-------etc.
```

Depending on where you are at with your playing, these different exercises will serve you in various ways. The more you do them, the more dexterous you will become. Bottom-line, more practice = better player, 100% of the time.

Alternate Picking Exercises Using Exercise 1

Now using exercise #1, practice alternate picking by using a consistent down/up stroke. Be very strict with this down/up stroke. (i.e. – down, up, down, up, down, up)

For some extra challenging practice, try using the following variations on the "1,2,3,4" picking exercise (use alternate - up/down – picking).

1234	2134	3124	4123
1243	2143	3142	4132
1324	2314	3214	4213
1342	2341	3241	4231
1423	2413	3412	4312
1432	2431	3421	4321

Chapter 6:

Basic Structure of Music Theory and Diatonic Harmony

- The musical alphabet goes from A to G (there is no "H, I, J" etc.)
- A half-step is the distance between one fret and the next on the ukulele
- A whole-step is equal to two half-steps or two frets distance
- A sharp (#) is when we raise a pitch by a half step
- A flat (b) is when we lower a pitch by a half step
- Every note has a sharp, except for B and E

So the musical alphabet reads like this: A A# B C C# D D# E F F# G G#

Chromatic Scale

Have you heard the vocal exercise "Do-Re-Mi-Fa-So-La-Ti-Do"? Those are the musical steps for the major scale...or "Do Re Mi" by Julie Andrews in "The Sound of Music"? That is a song based on the Major Scale steps. It is VERY important to learn the major scale if you want a good foundation for learning everything else on the ukulele. It is the basis of music theory which is the field of study that deals with the mechanics of music and how music works.

If W=whole step and H=half step then:

Major Scale = W W H W W W H

Scale steps:

1   2   3   4   5   6   7   8 (or 1)

Distance between notes:

W - W - H - W - W - W – H

Try this for yourself. Play any note within the first few frets of the uke (any string) and THEN follow with the pattern WWHWWWH and see how natural the major scale sounds. This formula allows you to play the major scale in ANY key quickly.

Definitions to Know:

Interval - the distance between two notes

Chord - 3 or more notes played together

Arpeggio - broken chord, or notes from a chord played apart from each other

Major Chord - 1st, 3rd, and 5th scale steps (notes) from the Major Scale 1, 3, 5

Minor Chord - 1st, b3^{rd}, and 5th scale steps (notes) from the Major Scale 1, b3, 5

Chapter 7:

How to Tune Your Ukulele

Keeping your ukulele in tune is extremely important. An out of tune ukulele like any instrument does not sound good, no matter who is playing it. With that being said, there are several ways that we can tune our ukulele.

Most ukuleles fall into the soprano/tenor/concert categories. The tuning of that instrument is G, C, E, A. with the A string being the string that is closest to the floor and the G string being the string that is closest to your head (when the uke is in playing position). If you are not playing with other musicians or say to a recording, then you could tune the instrument to itself.

What that means is each string is in relative pitch to the next. For example, let's say my G string is slightly flat and I tuned the rest of my strings to that G; then the entire ukulele will be in tune with itself but everything will be slightly flat to concert pitch. Concert pitch is a standard by which musicians tune their instruments so that when they show up at a gig, show or studio session there is a standard.

If you have a tuner already, then that makes things even easier. If you need a tuner, go to the bottom of the page at the following link to see the tuner that I use exclusively: http://www.yourguitarsage.com/faqs/guitar-gear. It's called the Snark and it's a very stealthy tuner for only a few dollars.

If you would like to tune by ear however check out this video tutorial that I created for you: http://www.yourguitarsage.com/tune-by-ear-ukulele

So now that we're in tune, let's keep moving! So again, when in proper playing position, the uke string that is closest in proximity to the ground is the A string. The string that is furthest in proximity to the ground is the G string.

So from top to bottom the strings are G, C, E, A. You'll need to know this to properly use a tuner or keyboard to tune your uke.

When a uke string is out of pitch, it will either be sharp (#), or flat (b). If a string is flat, then it's lower than our desired pitch and would need to be tightened in order to sharpen the pitch. If a string is sharp, then it's higher than our desired pitch and would need to be loosened in order to flatten the pitch.

Use your ear to determine which way the pitch is going when you are turning the tuning peg. Does it sound like its rising or falling? This basic concept of pitch is extremely important and only takes a minimal amount of attention to recognize.

So when you turn your tuning pegs and the pitch lowers, you are flattening the pitch of the string. When you turn your tuning pegs and the pitch raises, you are sharpening the pitch of the string.

Remember, ALWAYS be in tune!!! Your technique can be perfect along with your chords and melody, but if your instrument is out of tune, it will NOT sound good EVER....Tune up my friend!

If you don't have a tuner, that' OKAY! Watch this video to tune up!

http://www.yourguitarsage.com/tune-ukulele

Chapter 8:

How to Read Chord Stamps and the Top 24 Uke Chords

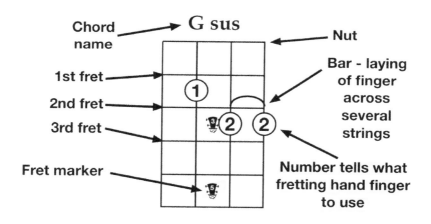

Chord name → G sus ← Nut

1st fret →

2nd fret →

3rd fret →

Bar - laying of finger across several strings

Number tells what fretting hand finger to use

Fret marker

How to Read Chord Stamps

The above diagram is called a chord stamp. It allows us to easily read chord shapes. Many chord stamp illustrations vary, but for our example let's go over the following:

The numbers (1, 2) represent the fretting hand finger that should be pressed down on that particular place on the neck. Index =1, Middle=2, Ring=3, Pinky=4. The bar (line) located on the third fret represents a "barred" fingering.

A bar is when you lay your finger across two or more strings, like a "bar". This can be tricky in the beginning, but don't overthink the process. Typically, a new player will only be able to bar 2 or 3 notes. As your hand gets stronger, you will be able to bar all 4 strings when necessary.
If you see an "X", that means "don't play that string", or "mute that string". It should not resonate (vibrate) when you play the chord. An "(X)" means that you can play this note, but you usually would not. Technically, this particular note could be played in the chord with-out any dissonance (disagreeable notes). If you play it, the chord will still sound harmonic (agreeable notes). Don't be too concerned with these however. We don't experience them too often on the uke.

How to Play the Top 24 Uke Chords

Playing chords can seem like a daunting task for new players, but remember EVERY player goes through this, so hang on! Firstly, remember the importance of playing on your fingertips. If you play on the pads of your fingers, you will NOT be able to play chords well. The only real exception to this is bar chords. For those, you often have to play on something other than your fingertips.

Observe your hand when you are playing. If something does not sound right, it's probably not!

Play with the specified fingers to start off. If you want to change fingerings after you have mastered these chords, then great. But for now, stick to the specified way and you will see the pay off. (Arpeggiate) Strum VERY slowly through the chord so that you can hear each note as it is being played. Being sloppy will only cheat you, so pay close attention.

When transitioning from one chord to the next, be aware of your fingers and which ones need to move where and what fingers stay (i.e.– when going from an F to an A minor, you could just lift your index finger up and keep the 2nd finger on the 2nd fret of the G string. " Get it?

Being aware of these small details will make you a very fast and efficient player. Since there are only a few basic chords that you will use often, take the time to notice how they look and feel on the fretboard.

Chapter 9:

Quick Uke Chords

A Minor

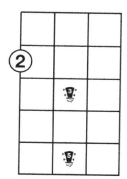

C Major

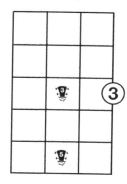

D Major

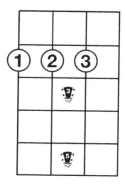

D Minor

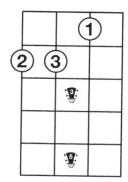

G Major

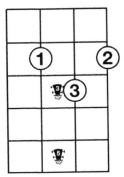

A Major

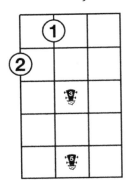

F Major

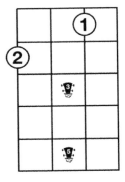

F7

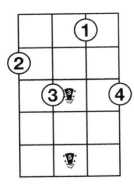

E Minor

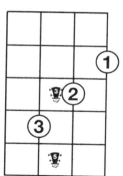

G7

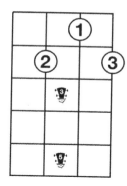

A7

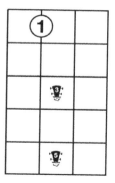

C7

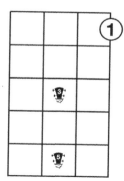

C Major 7

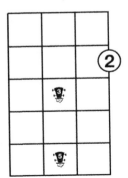

B7

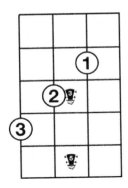

Am7

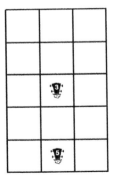

B Minor

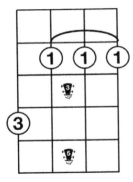

Eb Minor

Ab Minor

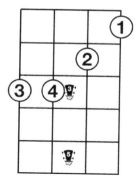
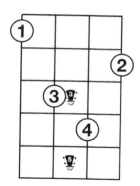

A#7

C# Major

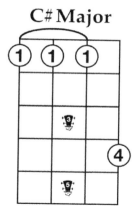

E Major

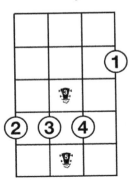

B Major

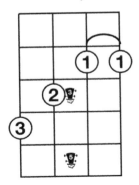

G#7

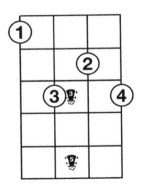

D7

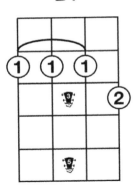

Chapter 10:

How the Ukulele Relates to the Guitar

For those guitar players out there, this section is really going to help you out. If you don't play guitar, you can skip this section.

When I first sat down with the ukulele, I said, "What is the quickest way that I can learn this instrument?" After noodling with it for a while I realized that many of the chord shapes and scales were similar to the guitar. If you've ever played a G chord on the ukulele before, you probably noticed that it looks a lot like a D chord from the guitar?

That's because a G chord is a perfect fourth (or 5 frets) up from a D chord (If you don't understand this part, that's okay. You WILL!) So here is how you will want to think about the ukulele. If you were to remove the two lowest strings (E and A) from the guitar, and capo the guitar at the fifth fret, you basically have the ukulele.

The only other thing that differs is that the top string of the ukulele (the G) would be one octave higher than this example (This applies to most ukes, except for baritone ukes which are tuned like the D, G, B and E strings on the guitar.) That high-pitched "G" string can be a little bit awkward for some guitar players as many players are used to "thumbing" the bass line on the lowest (pitched) strings.

So check this out!

Play a D chord on the guitar and then play a G chord on the ukulele. See how they look similar? Now play an A minor on the guitar and then play a D minor on the ukulele. Ignoring the top two strings on the guitar, can you see how the fingering is exactly the same? If not, take your time with this. I promise you that if you know chord and scale shapes on the guitar, then taking the time to understand this concept is crucial and invaluable to your mastering the uke. Let's try another.

Play an E minor on the guitar, then play an A minor on the ukulele. Again, ignoring the top two strings (E and A, or lowest in pitch) on the guitar can you see that the fingering is the same?

Once you get this concept, the ukulele fretboard will really start making sense. If you know certain scales on the guitar you will see that they are the same on the ukulele, only a perfect fourth higher (again, okay if you don't know this yet).

Remember though that the ukulele does NOT have 5th and 6th strings like the guitar, and THAT throws new uke players who are guitar players off a bit.

Take your time with this concept. It can be a bit to digest, especially if you are a newbie. However, the payoff is huge.

I use my guitar concepts ALL THE TIME on the uke and can play any guitar chord equivalent on the ukulele with just a little bit of "guitar" thinking.

Rome was not built in a day. Neither are great musicians. It takes thousands of hours to become a master musician. It takes lots of dedication to excel.

However, we can cover a TON of ground by having a good grasp of the fundamentals. THAT'S where we begin!

Chapter 11:

How to Read Chord Charts

Learning to read chord charts is fun and easy. It will open a new world of songs to you, as you will now be able to unlock the "code". As a teacher and studio guitar/ukulele player, I use charts all the time, especially for songs that I am not familiar with, or don't have the time and need for memorizing.

This method of playing music is not too dissimilar to preparing a speech and then reading it, or referring to your notes throughout the speech. Most bands that play together a lot don't use charts because they have played the songs enough times to have them memorized. However, studio musicians need to be able to play any song, without practice, instantly. This is where charts come in handy.

There are many chart types, but only a few that you see often. The type that we will be covering today, is the most common and most useful. The charts we will be covering are standard and "number" charts. There are several things that need to be covered before we can unlock these charts.

1. **Meter** - Most songs begin and end with the same "meter". Meter is defined as: rhythm that continuously repeats a single basic pattern. Most of today's music is in "4", which means that the basic pattern repeats every four beats. Most other tunes are in 8 or 6, where the pattern repeats every 8 or 6 beats respectively.

   Every now and then, you will find a song written in an "odd" time signature like 5 or 7. "Money" by Pink Floyd is in 7. If our chart says "in 4", that means that the pattern for the most part will repeat every four beats. Measures will also be four beats in length. If there is a strumming rhythm it will typically repeat every four beats as well. If you have trouble counting to the music, here are some things that might help.

   - Most songs emphasize the "1" beat. It's when most chords transition from one to another.

   - The snare drum (the very loud one that you can hear easily on recordings) is usually on the "2" and "4".

2. **Feel and Capo** - If the song needs a capo, it will typically be denoted like "Capo 3", etc. This would mean that you would put the capo at the 3rd fret. Using a capo, "transposes" the actual chords. Often, charts won't mention what the "feel" of the song is. That's no problem. Just capo where requested and act as if the capo is the "nut" of the ukulele.

   If you move the capo to the third fret, you will need to play your chords 3 frets higher than you would if you did not use a capo. I will often denote the feel of the song, especially if it's a "number" chart. This way you know what chord to play for the number represented. More on that later.

3. **Groupings** - Chords will be separated from each other when they represent a "measure". If a song is "In 4", you will see a chord separated by a space, and then another chord, etc. For the song, "Big Cheater" (in the chord charts section that follows), each chord represents 4 beats. So there would be a total of 16 beats for the

following chord progression (E- D C B7).
If a measure has more than one chord in it,
it's called a split measure and is denoted,
by an underline.

For example, in the song, "Hurry" (in the
charts section that follows), the 10th
measure of the verse is split C D. Since
this is still a measure of "4", "C" would get
two beats and "D" would get two beats. In
"Counting Song", the intro and verses are
all split. Since that song is in 4, each chord
would get two beats because they share the
measure. In the chorus it would be back to
our normal full measure of four beats per
chord. Sometimes you will see "hash"
marks over chords if it's not an evenly split
measure.

In "Hurts", you will find an "uneven"
measure, in the 1st bar (measure) of the
bridge. The "C" chord would normally be
held out for 3 beats, and the "D" for one
beat, but we have yet another notation to
consider. The "p" above the "D", means
that you "push" the D chord. Basically, you
just play it a little earlier than you would
normally play it. To be exact, you play the

"D" on the "and of 3", not on the 4. If we count 1+2+3+4+, the C is held for 1+2+3, and the D is played on the + of the 3 and held out for +4+.

This last part is a bit complex, so if you don't get it, don't worry. Come back to it though, because even though you won't run into it very often, you will hear a difference.

4. **Inversions** - (Typically inversions are not as prominent on ukulele, but are on guitar and piano) Inversions are chords that have another note from that chord that is played in the bass, instead of the "root" of the chord. C chord has a C in the root. D chord has a D in the root, etc. Sometimes you will see a chord symbol like "C/E" as we see in the 3rd measure of "Ellen".

Simply put, this is a C chord, with an "E" in the bass. However, when a / chord is represented, that usually means that another instrument (usually the bass) is playing that low note, instead of the root of the chord (i. e.-"C").

Other examples that you will see often times are G/B, which means a G chord, with a B in the bass. C/G is C chord with a G in the bass. D/F# is a D chord with an F# in the bass. If you don't quite get this section on inversions, don't worry. Inversions are rarely ever played on the uke.

Whenever you see a / chord, you can safely play the chord to the left of the slash. If it's a C/E, you just play a C chord. If it's a D/F#, you can just play the D. If you are playing with a bassist, he would usually play the lower note and your ear won't be searching for it. If you are playing by yourself (solo uke), you might find something "missing" with inversion chords, but that's also the nature of this simple but VERY cool instrument we call the ukulele.

Note:

Again for ukuleles, inversions are less of an issue because we only play with four strings and so our options are limited. Also, the top string on a guitar is the lowest string, while on the uke the top string is high and is not very useful for playing bass notes. So, when you see an inversion on a chart, you are safe to play the chord and skip out on the bass note.

5. **Number Charts** - Often times, studio musicians (especially in Nashville) will prefer a "number chart". These charts refer to numbers instead of letters. The reason that studio players like these types of charts is that they are easy to transpose (change keys). Refer to the "number system matrix" in the next chapter to see where I am getting these chords from.

For "Hurry", the 1 represents the G and the 6 represents an E. However, there is a minus (-) after the E. That means that you play the chord as an E minor or E-. The fifth measure of the verse is a 4, which in the key of G is a C chord.

The sixth measure is a 5, which in the key of G is a D. If we were in the studio and the singer wanted to try this in the key of C, instead of G, we wouldn't have to rewrite our charts. We would just have to "think" in the key or feel of C. In this scenario, the 1 would be a C, the 6- would be an A-, the 4 would be an F and the 5 would be a G.

Another reason that we might want to change keys (other than the singer), is playing ease. This song is easier played with a G feel, so that our 5 chord is a D instead of an F (in the key of C). However, in the 14th measure of the 1st verse, we find a 3-. In C, that would be an E-, which is an easy chord to play. In G, the 3- would be a B-, which is a bar chord and a more difficult chord to play. Using the capo helps us to limit bar chords, but sometimes they are unavoidable. Everything else however is consistent between number charts and standard charts. To summarize, number charts substitute numbers instead of letters.

6. **Symbols and Notation** - Since charts are condensed versions of actual music, there is often much left to the imagination. We can't hear a piece of music. It is lifeless, until a musician brings it to life! Symbols and notation help musicians get a better idea of what the composer or arranger wants, like road signs do when we drive. Since these are fairly impromptu and different from each chart writer to the next, sometimes you just have to use common sense (i.e.-if a chorus is followed by 3x, it most likely signifies that you should play the chorus three times).

However, you will see these symbols "[:"

and ":]" or something similar fairly often. These denote a repeated section of music. If you were to see, "[: E-C G D:]", you would play E-, C, G and D and then repeat it. If the ":]" were followed by a 3x, you would play for a total of three times.

7. **How to Practice** - If you are still new to chords and moving between them, it's best to first practice your transitions. To do this, move your fretting hand (relax the strum hand) back and forth between two chords. Just toggle back and forth without strumming. Try this for a bit with all the chord transitions in a song.

   Once you get the left hand "working", you can strum to make sure the chords sound nicely. Remember that every great player has struggled with the same chords that you and I struggle with.

   DON'T GIVE UP!!!

   Just be observant to your hands when you hear something that's not right. Once you have the transitions down, it's best to play the chord on the "1" and hold it out for the full measure or four beats (if the song is in 4). Often times this is called a "diamond" or whole note.

You will see this written in many of my charts when a chord is to be held out for a full measure. Playing in "diamonds" will get your internal metronome (clock) in better sync with the music. Once you get the "feel" of diamonds, you can start strumming on each single beat. If you know what the strumming rhythm of the song is, you could then practice that, but not before getting the "diamonds" and single note strums down. Here is the breakdown for practicing these charts:

1. **Transitions**

2. **Diamonds**

3. **Single beat strums**

4. **Actual strumming rhythm of song**

In summary, charts will allow you to play music that you have never played before. At first your reading will be slower, just like it was when you learned to read a book. Then as the months and years progressed, so did your reading ability. Sooner than later, you will be able to look at a chart and play it correctly the first time, just like reading a book. Practice, practice, practice and have fun!!!

Chapter 12:

Use This Number System Matrix to Help You Simplify Your Understanding of Music

I have included a section for minor keys below the major keys, but MANY musicians will still chart and think about songs from the major key perspective, whether the song is minor or not. Notice the song "Big Cheater" in the charts chapter later in the book. The song is actually in the key of E minor (where technically the 1 is the E minor). However, many musicians including myself will think of the song in G, while emphasizing the 6-. Either way is correct.

Major	1	2	3	4	5	6	7
Quality	Maj	Min	Min	Maj	Maj	Min	Dim
Key of A	A	B-	C#-	D	E	F#-	G#°
Key of B	B	C#-	D#-	E	F#	G#-	A#°
Key of C	C	D-	E-	F	G	A-	B°
Key of D	D	E-	F#-	G	A	B-	C#°
Key of E	E	F#-	G#-	A	B	C#-	D#°
Key of F	F	G-	A-	Bb	C	D-	E°
Key of G	G	A-	B-	C	D	E-	F#°
Minor	1	2	3	4	5	6	7
Quality	Min	Dim	Maj	Min	Min	Maj	Maj
Key of A-	A-	B°	C	D-	E-	F	G
Key of B-	B-	C#°	D	E-	F#-	G	A
Key of C-	C-	D°	Eb	F-	G-	Ab	Bb
Key of D-	D-	E°	F	G-	A-	Bb	C
Key of E-	E-	F#°	G	A-	B-	C	D
Key of F-	F-	G°	Ab	Bb-	C-	Db	Eb
Key of G-	G-	A°	Bb	C-	D-	Eb	F

Chapter 13:

Talent vs. Practice

Have you ever seen your favorite musician totally dominate their instrument without even seemingly trying?

Do you think they got that way because they were lucky, or because they were born into it?

Let me both disappoint and liberate you at the same time with the answer. **One player isn't any luckier than another or born into playing easier than another.** If you were to take the top musicians of each genre and find out how much they have practiced and how much they continually practice, it would be quite mind boggling.

Is it a coincidence that only the great players are the ones that practice so much?

Obviously, you can see where I'm headed with this. Musicians, who have been playing for a long time and still have not progressed past a certain point, have not done so because of lack of talent; they've not done so because of their <u>lack of</u>

<u>practice!</u>

If it makes you feel better to believe that musicians like Jimi Hendrix or Eric Clapton were born with a gift that you were not born with, then believe away only to the detriment of your own playing.

However, it's NOT the truth and that type of small thinking will hinder your playing greatly. Don't believe the lie!

This is a subject that is rarely addressed or, often times, misunderstood completely, EVEN by top musicians. The definition of "talent" is a <u>natural aptitude or skill</u>. As far as practice goes, we all know what practice is and that doing more of it makes us better at whatever skill we are trying to improve. I know I'm going to step on some toes with this portion of the book, but bear with me because <u>I promise you</u> that what I am going to share with you in this section will only empower you to become the best player that <u>you</u> allow yourself to be.

Simply put, the point of this section is that the belief that you must be born talented or have some natural inclination to excel above others is not only completely false, but also extremely limiting to your playing... and your life!

Many people believe so fervently in this idea of an innate need for talent – as opposed to sheer practice – that they talk themselves right out of excellence!

Defenders of the talent theory like to use examples of great icons that excel in a particular field or genre and say "there, you can't tell me that they are not talented!" They *assume* that the person was simply born with the ability they are displaying in their excellent performance.

This assumption, however, is very insulting and negates the thousands – or even tens of thousands of hours – that a person has spent "perfecting" their craft.

What do Jimi Hendrix, Amadeus Mozart, Michael Jordan and Nikola Tesla all have in common?

Well, depending on who you ask, some might say they were gifted or talented. Others, who have taken the time to step back, will realize that their gains are because of dedication, innovation, organization and perseverance. They understand that **the more one practices, the better one**

gets.

Now I know that concept sounds logical, but see if you can step outside yourself for a moment and watch yourself slip into the "talent camp" when something appears to be out of your reach.

What I'm saying is, and I know this from personal experience because I used to do it often, it's easy to look at someone who has **"mastered his craft"** and say that they have some leg up on you. I've done it many times throughout my life. I used to do it more often with musicians, but my love of illusions (magic), martial arts, etc., have also made me assume that somebody had a hidden key that I was not able to find.

I have played music for several decades now, have learned thousands of songs and have attempted to imitate hundreds of players. I have seen success in all of these areas. I've had many people comment on how "talented" I am. The funny thing is, when I started playing uke/guitar/bass, I was *TERRIBLE!* Why is that?

It is that way because everybody is terrible when they just pick up their instrument! It's just that some folks forgot the process and how long it actually took them. Jimi Hendrix was not good when he first picked up the guitar! Amadeus Mozart was not good when he first played the piano!

Are you getting the picture?

We would be much better off to replace the word talent with perseverance. Now that is a pill I can swallow! If someone said to me "the reason that a particular player does not play as well as Jimi Hendrix is because he doesn't have the talent," I would <u>never</u> concur. If someone said to me, "the reason that someone does not play as well as Jimi Hendrix is because they don't have the same perseverance that he had," I would wholeheartedly agree!

Perhaps to define it better, instead of the word perseverance we could even replace it with "efficient practice time." Now how unromantic is that? I know! It kind of makes you want to call it "talent" again right? How much cooler to think that we would not have to work and that we could just be born into such a thing?

Let's not fall into that trap. It's lame, it's lazy and it's <u>NOT the truth</u>.

Jimi Hendrix started playing music somewhere

around 10 years old. If he were so "talented", he would not have had to practice so much? Why didn't we hear of him "breaking into" the music scene at 10 or 11? What about Amadeus Mozart, Michael Jordan and Nikola Tesla? Mozart was known to utterly surround himself with music. He was constantly immersed in it from a very young age.

It's true that some people catch "the music bug" earlier than others, giving them several years more practice than others. That is a truism that you can't escape.

If someone starts playing ukulele at age 4 as opposed to another that started at age 14, when both reach the age of 15 the one uke player will have been practicing for 11 years while the other will have been practicing for one year. It's simple math. Can you see which player might sound better? Is this what we're calling talented?

I heard a story about Michael Jordan where he did not make the high school basketball team because he SUCKED. YES, that Michael Jordan!

However he was <u>determined</u> to play basketball. So he got that basketball out and started shooting hoops and still sucked for a bit, until continuous "suckyness" turned into kind of sucking, which turned into not so sucky, which turned into kind of good, which turned into pretty good, which turned into the best NBA basketball player to ever grace the courts! WHEW!!!

Have you got it yet? It DOES NOT happen overnight! He made his own destiny by being determined and practicing. In essence he became talented.

What about Nikola Tesla? Who the heck is that you ask? He's the guy that invented the light bulb. Not Edison as history books tell us. Yep, pretty important! He also invented hundreds of other things that we use today. Look him up on Google if you want to see a man who has changed the lives of billions of people.

When Tesla was creating the light bulb he used hundreds of different filaments before finding the right one. The filament of the light bulb is that little thing in the middle that glows.

He used everything under the sun including horsehair but to no avail. Finally he got it right. Enter sarcastic Sage voice, "Boy, that talented Tesla. He is just so lucky. Stuff just comes to him SOOO easily." Can you see how insulting that is when he worked his hind end off to create such a technology?

In fact, it was Thomas Edison "Teslas one time boss" who said, "Genius is 1% inspiration and 99% perspiration" or in my words 1% talent and 99% practice. So that little 1% seed that was dropped into Jimi Hendrix, Amadeus Mozart, Michael Jordan, Nikola Tesla and YOU, must be watered and fed and given all the conditions to make that seed grow into fruition. That's the harder part.

Seeds like that are dropped all day long but rarely do they find fertile ground. If you've gotten this far in my diatribe, I would guess YOU are fertile ground and are going to run with this information.

There is NO-thing stopping YOU from becoming the next Mozart or Eddie Van Halen IF you practice like they did. THAT'S the tricky part. You were already born into this world with the ability to succeed, but you MUST water the seed!

Now that you know this, I want you to be aware of how you view great accomplishments. It does take a little bit of the wonderment away, but empowers you to create that wonderment for yourself. There is no task too great, or goal too lofty that you cannot attain if properly mapped out and walked through step-by-step.

This is not a pep talk, as I rarely have time for pep talks. This is a truism and is good news for those of us that are willing to work hard and smart. It's *bad news* for those that are waiting for talent or the Publisher's Clearinghouse sweepstakes guy to deliver a big check to their front door.

Now, **<u>DON'T</u>** go easy on yourself. Go practice as if you are the next Amadeus Mozart, because you ARE!

Chapter 14:

Where the Notes Fall on the Fretboard

It's not often that uke players read from sheet music. In fact, I never do, BUT there is nothing to say you can't! AND knowing the basics will help fill in some gaps and make you that much better of a musician!

The lines below represent standard musical notation. We won't be using standard musical notation in this manual, but the information is very useful when trying to decipher sheet music. As you can see in the diagrams below, each line and space is represented by a letter from our musical alphabet A-G.

The lines from the bottom to the top are **EGBDF**. The traditional way to memorize this is: **E**very, **G**ood, **B**oy, **Do**es, Fine. The spaces are easy. From the lowest to the top it's **F, A, C, E.**

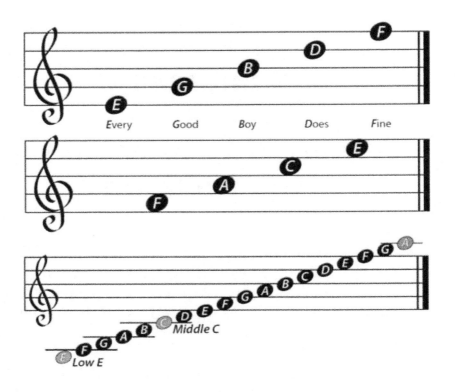

Every   Good   Boy   Does   Fine

In musical notation, you would see a "#" or " ♭ " before that note, if you are supposed to play a sharp or flat. Get it? To see where the sharps and flats are, see the diagrams in this chapter. Sharps are only represented here, but every sharped note is also a flattened note from the note above. For example, an A# is also a B ♭ . Conversely a D ♭ would be a C#.

Chromatic Scale

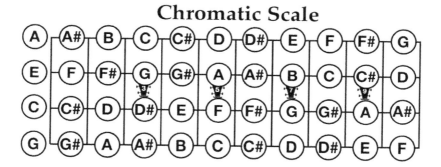

Chapter 15:

How to Conquer the Bar Chords in Just Two Easy-to-follow Steps

Bar chords, also known as *barre chords*, are any chord that requires at least one finger to press down multiple strings simultaneously (at the same time). Bar chords allow players to play chords that are not restricted to the open strings. Bar chords are known as movable chords as each form can be moved up and down the neck in a linear fashion. That is, one bar chord formation will allow the player to play a chord in any key by merely moving it up or down the neck.

Bar chords can be used **in conjunction with open chords or with other bar chords**. Bar chords are sometimes necessary when a song requires a chord to be played that cannot otherwise be played open. Any chord played in the open position can be replicated as a bar chord further up the neck, given of course that the player has built the strength and dexterity to do so.

"So hold on Erich! You are saying that *anything* I play in the open position can be played further up the neck in bar chord fashion to produce the same chord in every other key?" Yes! That one concept alone will open up your playing quite a bit. That means that many of those open chords that you already know are going to become our patterns or "templates" for the first set of bar chords that you should learn.

As you probably know already from watching my instructional videos on my YouTube channels, many of my lessons are based around open chords and the use of a capo. I try to keep things as simple as possible when teaching.

My philosophy is, *"there's no need in complicating something that's not complicated."* There are plenty of intricate music parts that cannot be simplified. In those cases there is no way around it; however, sometimes even the simplest of songs call for bar chords and there's no way around that, either.

The capo can be used to *limit bar chords* or change the forms of the open chords that you would use, but sometimes you just have to play a bar chord. In those cases wouldn't it be nice to have that ability?

Some players might skip this section fearing the "dreaded" bar chords. While others may feel that their playing does not lack without bar chords. But that's not you! You want to excel as a musician and I am going to help you!

Having said all of that, bar chords are challenging for "ukers" who have never played them. Remember that you *and your hands* are learning a new concept! Please be patient with yourself during this process and understand that **everyone** has difficulty with bar chords in the beginning.

I have taught hundreds of students over several decades and have never met a student, even my best, who got this concept immediately. **So be encouraged**, take your time, and enjoy the process.

There are many bar chords, but here we will only be illustrating the ones that you will use the most. In fact, we will be looking at 10 bar chord shapes that we will derive from 10 open chord shapes, most of which you know already. Since these shapes are movable, moving them up the fretboard one fret at a time will add over 100 new chords to your chord vocabulary!

The specific flavored bar chords that we will be looking at are major, minor, 7 and minor 7 chords Knowing this ninja trick will allow you to play millions of songs and rarely, if ever, get stumped about a chord.

The more you practice them, the faster and better you will become.

I like to break the subject of bar chords down into two sections:

1. Understanding the forms

2. Playing the chords

Step One: Understanding the Forms with This Simple to Use Method

Check out the bar chord diagrams that follow the description below. Now locate the first major chord which is a "C major". If we were to capo our ukulele at the first fret and then proceed to play a C major form we would essentially be playing this chord as a bar chord except the capo would be doing the bar that our first finger would normally do.

Now, if we took the capo off and laid our first finger across strings G, C, and E, and placed our pinky at the fourth fret we would then be playing our first bar chord form. This bar chord form is based off of the open C major chord, so it's known as the "C major" bar chord form. However, since this whole form has been moved up a half a step, the chord is no longer C major but is in fact a C# major.

If we took that same exact form and moved up yet another half-step, we would now have a D major bar chord. Moving that chord form one fret up each time would give you yet another major chord form moving up the neck "chromatically". So, our chromatic scale (all the notes in the musical spectrum) goes: A, A#, B, **C**, C#, D, D#, E, F, F#, G, G#.

So moving to the right of this scale will give you the root or letter name of each chord as you move up the ukulele neck in half-steps. Remember that a half-step is the distance between one fret and the next.

So to reiterate, any chord that you play in the open position (chord where open strings are prominent) can be moved up the neck in half steps utilizing the bar chord technique.

Get it? I knew you would!

Now that you understand where the forms come from and how they move about the fretboard, let's talk about how to play them.

Chord forms follow this chapter.

Step Two: Discover the Secret to Playing Easy Bar Chords

Understanding how the chords move about the fretboard and <u>actually playing</u> the chords are two totally different things. When playing bar chords, lazy or poor technique will quickly limit you. There are a lot of other techniques - like playing single notes - which "ukers" can "fudge," even with poor technique. Not so much with bar chords... so trust me through this process. No one gets this right off the bat; it is a learned technique that the more you do, the better you become. Now that we have that excuse out of the way, *let's do this thing!*

As someone new to playing bar chords, the following points are of utmost importance! If you find yourself having difficulty, make sure you are aware of the following:

1. The finger that does the barring, MUST either be perfectly straight, or better yet hyper-extended.

    Here is a great exercise: Lift your fretting hand up and view your index finger from the side. While viewing it from the side, straighten the finger. Now go beyond that and see if you can't slightly bend the finger backwards.

Obviously, our knuckles don't allow us to bend the finger back too far, but just that little bit is what we call hyper-extended. In this hyper-extended position, your finger is ideally situated for evenly distributing the weight of that finger across all the strings in your bar chord. Even if your finger is perfectly straight, this is a great place to start. I usually tell my students to hyper-extend that finger a little bit because I know the natural tendency is to bend it the other way - which is awesome if you want your bar chords to sound like poo!

If the barring finger is flexed or bent in its natural direction - even the slightest bit - during the bar chord, you *most likely* will have some unwanted muted notes.

2. In order to have that straight or hyper-extended barring finger, we need to make sure that the pad of our thumb is on the back of the neck closer towards the bottom part and not lazily hanging over the top of the neck. That may be fine for melody

notes and open chords from time to time, but it's a sure-fire way to mess up your bar chords. ***So don't do it!***

3. Keeping your thumb on the back of the neck (at least in the early stages of learning the uke) should allow for some space between the palm of your hand and bottom of the neck. Again, at least in the beginning, you want to make sure that space is there, otherwise you will have difficulty with your bar chords.

4. For the fingers that are not barring, but are playing individual notes, make sure that those fingers are playing directly on the fingertips and not on the pads. This is extremely important! Seriously, for my students that are playing sloppy bar chords or claim that they can't play them at all, they are always breaking one of these rules... or several. "So listen to me now and believe me later." For those other fingers remember, "FINGERTIPS! FINGERTIPS! FINGERTIPS!"

For now, the trick will be to bar your barring finger properly, while properly playing on the fingertips of all the other fingers. If you don't give up and practice, YOU WILL GET IT!!

Practice, practice, practice!! You've heard me say it and you'll keep hearing me say it! You are only as good as how long and how well you are practicing! No one is a "natural" at this; anyone who desires this skill must practice it.

Bar Chord Forms for Ukulele

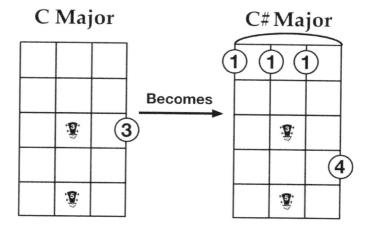

F Major → F# Major

A Major → A# Major

A Minor → A# Minor

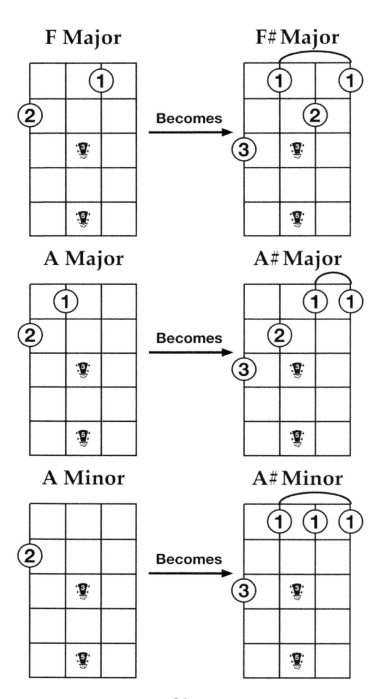

94

D Minor

D# Minor

G Minor

G# Minor

C7

C#7

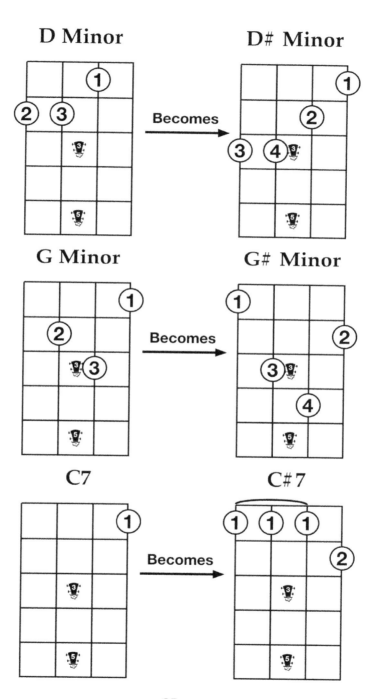

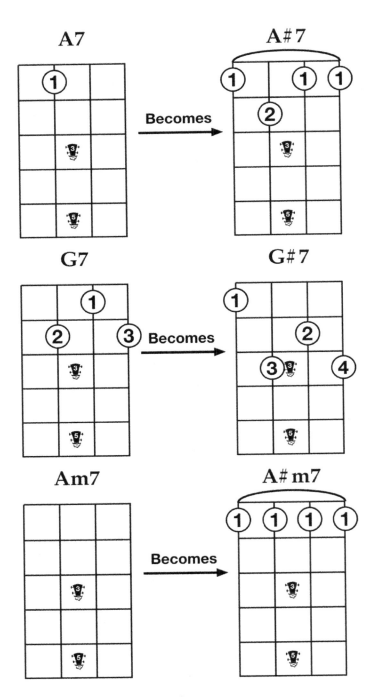

Chapter 16:

Understanding How to Change Keys with the Capo Quickly and Easily

A **capo** (pronounced "cape-o") is a movable bar attached to the fingerboard of a fretted instrument to uniformly raise the pitch of all the strings. Capos allow us to play songs in different keys, without altering our fingering. The musical alphabet is as follows:

A   A#   B   C   C#   D   D#   E   F   F#   G   G#

Let's say we have a song that is in G (Major), and the chords are G, C, A- and D. If we want to transpose (change keys) that song up a half step (1 fret), then we would place the capo at the 1 fret and move our chords up 1 fret as well. Doing this allows us to play in our new key of G#, but still allows us to play in a "feel" of G.

If we did NOT use the capo, we would have to play four bar chords (G#, C#, A#- and D#), which is no fun. With our capo at the 1st fret, we will have transposed to G#, without having to play all those pesky bar chords. This will also allow us to free up some fingers to add ornamental parts to a once basic chord progression.

When I chart a song, I will notate at the top of the page if and where you should put the capo, and often what "feel" the song will be in. For the song example in the above paragraph, I would notate "Capo 1(G feel)."

G, C and D are the easier "feels" to play songs in. You will often find songs that are in another key, but use a capo and follow the chord structures of those easier keys. It's easy to transpose, using the number system matrix that I have created.

However, you don't need to use this chart, if you can work a little basic math. If you use the musical alphabet above, you could capo 1 (G feel) to play in G#. If you want to play in the key of A, with a "G feel", capo at the 2nd fret. To play in the key of B, with a "G feel", capo at the 4th fret.

Similarly, you can do this for keys C and D. If you want to play in the key of D, but with a "C feel", capo at the 2nd fret. This will make more sense when you see the upcoming "capo key chart."

What Type of Capo Should You Buy?

As you may know, I am a guitar player as well. I use several types of guitar capos when I don't care to play bar chords. There are capos specifically made for the ukulele, but I have found that most of my guitar capos work just as well.

My favorite brands are Shubb, Kyser and G7th. The Shubb and G7th are adjustable, whereas the Kyser is "clamp-styled". The Kyser will easily clamp to your headstock when not in use, whereas the Shubb and G7th don't clamp on as easily. The adjustable Shubb and G7th are nice because they allow for the least amount of needed pressure on the strings, which keeps them from going out of tune.

The Kyser, in my opinion, tends to put ukes out of tune just a wee bit. So the Kyser is great for the quick "on and off" of live acoustic gigs, however I use the G7th and Shubb a lot in the studio.

Chapter 17:

Capo Key Chart

Capo Key Chart

Capo on Fret Number	C	G	D	A	E
no capo / open	C	G	D	A	E
1	C#	G#	D#	A#	F
2	D	A	E	B	F#
3	D#	A#	F	C	G
4	E	B	F#	C#	G#
5	F	C	G	D	A
6	F#	C#	G#	D#	A#
7	G	D	A	E	B
8	G#	D#	A#	F	C
9	A	E	B	F#	C#

Chapter 18:

How to Master Uke Strumming Quickly and Easily

Strumming the uke can be frustrating if you are not shown the proper way to think and if you don't allow yourself some time to master some basic rhythm skills. Here are some fundamental concepts that I want you to think about when practicing strumming.

1. Mute the uke strings with your fretting hand (if you are a "righty," this would be your left hand). This will allow you to focus all of your attention on your strum.

2. *For the following exercises*, the numbers will **ALWAYS** be "down strums" (strumming towards the floor), while the "+" symbol (also known as the "and" of the beat) will **ALWAYS** be an "up strum." This is the KEY to good strumming. Be diligent with this basic principle.

3. Each strum should be equal distance from the last. If you are counting 1 + 2 + 3 + 4 +, the count should be smooth and even like a watch or clock ticking (unless you are "swinging the beat," which is not recommended before learning a basic straight strum). A swing rhythm sounds more like a heart-beat and is used often in blues music.

4. Say the rhythm out loud, slowly. Once you get the idea, try to say that same rhythm in a seamless "loop" (meaning, don't stop at the end of the 4+). Keep counting!! Once you get the hang of this, it should stream together like 1 + 2 + 3 + 4 + 1 + 2 + 3 + 4 + 1 + 2 + 3 + 4 +

5. Once you can count it smoothly like this, strum it slowly and steadily. If you are new to strumming, try the very first strum, which is 4 down strums on the down beats.

6. When the strum calls for a space or void like 1   2 + 3 + 4+ or 1 + 2 + 3   4+, your hand should STILL move as if it were going to hit the strings. This way your down strums will always be where your down beats are and your up strums will be where

your up beats are.

For a video representation of this technique, check out:
http://www.yourguitarsage.com/ukulele-strumming-lesson

NOW for the exercises! For this study, take it slow and go through ALL levels in order.

Level 1

1		2		3		4	
1	+	2	+	3	+	4	+
1	+	2	+	3	+	4	
1	+	2	+	3		4	+
1	+	2		3	+	4	+
1		2	+	3	+	4	+

Level 2

1		2		3		4	
1	+	2		3	+	4	
1		2		3	+	4	+
1	+	2	+	3		4	
1		2	+	3	+	4	
1	+	2		3		4	+
1		2	+	3		4	+

Level 3

1		2		3		4	
1	+	2	+	3			+
1	+	2	+		+	4	+
1	+		+	3		4	+
	+	2	+	3		4	+

Level 4

1	+	2	+		+		+
1	+		+		+	4	+
	+		+	3	+	4	+
1	+		+	3	+		+
	+	2	+		+	4	+

Level 5

1		2	+		+		+
1	+		+		+		+
	+		+		+		+
1		2	+	3			+
1		2	+		+	4	+

Remember to TAKE IT SLOW and don't get the fretting hand involved until you feel VERY consistent about the strumming hand. With diligent time and practice you will get REALLY good at this.

Chapter 19:

How to Read Ukulele Tablature - It's Much Easier than You Think – Part 2

Previously in this book we learned the basics of tablature. Now that we understand that and have some other skills sets under our fingers and in our minds, let's further investigate this language of tablature.

Tablature Symbols and Their Related Techniques

Remember how I said tablature provides a lot of detail? The following are tablature symbols that represent various techniques. Since new techniques are being discovered all the time, this is not an exhaustive list.

- H – hammer-on
- P – pull-off
- B – bend string
- / – slide up

- \ – slide down
- V – vibrato (sometimes written as ~)
- T- pick hand tap
- Harm. – natural harmonic
- A.H. – artificial harmonic
- A.T. – tapped harmonic
- Tr – trill
- T – tap
- TP or 3 diagonal lines underneath a note – tremolo picking
- PM – Palm muting
- X – on rhythm, slash represents muted strum

Hammer On

A "**hammer-on**" is a technique performed by sharply bringing a fretting-hand finger down on the fingerboard behind a fret causing a note to sound. For our example here, you would pick the open string and hammer the 2nd or 3rd fret as indicated. Hammer-ons might feel awkward at first, but they are easily mastered with practice. As the name indicates, hammer your finger in a quick snapping motion so that the string does not have time to fade out. A snappy hammer-on will vibrate the string almost as much as a strong picking.

By the way, this is the A minor pentatonic or C major pentatonic scale that you are about to play.

```
1st string or A----------------------------0-h-3-----thin string
2nd string or E------------------0-h-3------------
3rd string or C-----------0-h-2-------------------
4th string or G---0-h-2--------------------------
```

Pull-Off

A "**pull-off**" is the opposite of a hammer-on. A pull-off is a technique performed by plucking a string by "pulling" the string off the fingerboard with one of the fingers being used to fret the note. For our example here, you would pick the 2nd or 3rd fret as indicated and pull-off to the open string. Pull-offs can also be a little awkward at first but with practice can be mastered. As its name indicates, pulling your finger off the fingerboard in a snapping motion causes the string to vibrate as if picked.

```
1st string or A--3-p-0----------------------------- thin string
2nd string or E----------3-p-0---------------------
3rd string or C--------------------2-p-0-----------
4th string or G----------------------------2-p-0----
```

111

Bend

A **bend** is represented by the symbol 'b' or an arrow bending up or down. A bend occurs when the musician physically pushes the string across the fretboard causing a change in pitch. Since bends vary in duration and style, often times each arrow is illustrated differently. Often times, the word "full", or "1/2" will be written along with this, indicating that the note should be bent up either one whole-step or one half-step. Bends of larger intervals can occur. Typically the actual pitch change will be denoted.

```
1st string or A—3b-(full) ------------------------ thin string
2nd string or E----------------2b-(1/2)-----------
3rd string or C------------------------------------
4th string or G------------------------------------
```

Slide-Up/Slide-Down

A **slide-down** is represented by the symbol "/". A slide-up occurs when a note is picked and slid up to another note. The second note is not picked, but instead is still vibrating from the previous pick and the agitation of the string during the slide. Opposite of a slide-up, a slide-down is represented by the symbol '\'. A slide-down occurs when a note is picked and slid down to another note. Typically, mastering the slide-down takes more time than mastering the slide-up.

```
1ˢᵗ string or A—3/5 ----------------------------- thin string
2ⁿᵈ string or E----------3/5 ---------------------
3ʳᵈ string or C--------------------4\2 ------------
4ᵗʰ string or G-------------------------5\2---
```

Vibrato

Vibrato is a pulsating effect by bending the string in a rhythmic fashion. This technique is created by bending the string up and down rhythmically or shaking the string/neck. This effect works best after a string is picked. A vibrato is usually represented by 'v' or '~'.

```
1ˢᵗ string or A—5v ------------------------------- thin string
2ⁿᵈ string or E------------5~~~~~~~-------------
3ʳᵈ string or C--------------------------------------
4ᵗʰ string or G--------------------------------------
```

Tapping

The **tapping** technique is similar to a hammer-on, except it is done with the picking hand. It is almost always followed by a pull-off. The technique is performed when the picking hand taps the string hard enough to push the string against the fret creating a note to sound at that specific fret.

```
1st string or A—7(t)-p-o----------------------------thin string
2nd string or E---------7(t)-p-o-------------------
3rd string or C------------------------------------
4th string or G------------------------------------
```

Harmonic (Natural)

A **harmonic** is a "chimed" string. This technique is produced by plucking the string while lightly touching the string over the indicated fret. The fret is not actually played in the traditional sense. When done correctly, a chime-like sound will be produced.

Harmonic (Artificial)

Artificial harmonics are also known as a pseudo-harmonics, pinch-harmonics or "squealies." This technique requires allowing the string to lightly graze the side of your thumb after picking it. Don't try to over-think the process. When you pick a note, allow your thumb to keep traveling towards the string until it mutes it.

Once you get the hang of that, try letting the thumb just barely touch the string. If done properly, you will hear a slight chime. Pseudo-harmonics are typically easier to produce on lower pitched strings and lower fretted notes; however, if the proper technique is used, an artificial harmonic can be produced on any picked note.

This technique is rarely ever used with the ukulele, but you will see it in tablature however, especially guitar tablature.

Trill

The term "**trill**" is typically used when referring to a continuous back-and-forth, hammer-on and pull-off of two notes. Mastering the hammer-on and pull-off techniques will allow for quick and precise trills.

Tremolo Picking

Tremolo picking refers to fast, repetitive picking on one note. This technique is achieved by quickly picking a note up and down. Typically tremolo picking refers to single notes (not chords).

Palm Muting

Palm muting refers to the muting of strings with the picking hand in order to create a percussive or staccato (sharp attack) effect on notes or chords. This technique is achieved by placing the picking hand palm on the bridge of the uke just where the strings meet the bridge. Backing the hand further towards the bridge creates a more standard, open sound. Moving the hand slightly closer to the strings will create a tighter, more closed-type sound. This technique can be used for all genres of music but is most prevalent in rock.

Although many of these techniques are not often used on the ukulele, you will see the notations in many tabs.

Chapter 20:

Fail Proof Method for Conquering Fingerpicking

Fingerpicking is the use of one's fingers to strike or pluck the strings instead of using a pick (plectrum). This technique is widely used in classical, flamenco, Spanish and folk music; however, it has also been used in nearly every genre of music - including pop and rock.

Fingerpicking allows the player to be more selective regarding what strings should sound when playing the uke polyphonically (multiple simultaneous notes).

When reading music that uses fingerpicking, you may see the term "PIMA" or the initials P, I, M or A used. PIMA is an acrostic for the thumb and the first three fingers of the right hand. Because of its length, the pinky is often times not used and not necessary when playing the ukulele. PIMA is often utilized to indicate which fingers to use in picking. The traditional Spanish words that we derive those letters from are:

Pulgar = Thumb
Indice = Fore Finger
Medio = Middle Finger
Anular = Ring Finger

I know! I don't speak Spanish either. It's certainly a lovely language, but we need something else to help us remember the fingers. Here's how to think about them.

- For P, think pick - or if you're in the UK, they call it a plectrum.

- For I, think of the index finger

- For M, think of the middle finger

- For A, think of the anniversary (ring) finger

Fingerpicking, like any other technique that we are going to study, requires practice, attention and a lot of patience. This is a technique that feels awkward at first and too, with time and discipline, miraculously gets easier. If the definition of an arpeggio is a broken chord or a chord where the notes are played independently of each other, then you are about to play a lot of arpeggios.

Until you get more comfortable with the fingerpicking hand playing the prescribed patterns, it's extremely important that you focus all of your attention on the fingerpicking and not the fretting.

So, let your fretting hand relax. You won't be using it to start off here. Now with your fingerpicking hand, place your thumb (P) on the 4th string, your index finger (I) on the third string, your middle finger (M) on the second string and your ring finger (A) on the first string. Now, just rest your fingers there for a moment. I want you to indelibly (forever etched in your mind) picture how your fingers are sitting on the strings. Remember this one concept and fingerpicking will almost never be an issue for you. How your fingers are sitting on the strings is the basis of 99% of the fingerpicking that you will encounter.

Now, notice the two headings on the fingerpicking exercise page that follow this description: "Songs in 4" and "Songs in 6".

The first example under "Songs in 4" says PIMA. That means if the song count is 1, 2, 3, 4, you would pick P, I, M, A, or thumb, index, middle, ring. You get it? I knew you would... you're smart like that. Once you get this basic feel down, work your way down the list. This may take you an hour or all week. There is no crime in over practicing. It will only make you more ninja-like!

So the next exercise would be P, I, A, M, and so on. Practice each exercise for a few minutes. This will assure that you have a good feel before moving to the next exercise. When you're done with that list, move to the next list, where you will find other finger combinations. When you see two finger letters underneath a beat, both of those fingers should be played simultaneously (at the same time). On the 3rd list we have more of the same, only this time the thumb shares in the combination pick. This is what is referred to as a pinch-pick. It is called a pinch-pick because the motion looks much like a pinch if executed properly. When you come to this list, this section will make more sense.

Fingerpicking can be done in any time signature. *However*, 4/4 and 6/8 are by far the most common. In fact, they will make up the majority of the songs that you encounter. To get you started, I have included 28 exercise patterns. Some of these patterns you will never use, but many of them you will. However, practicing each one will help undo any mental blocks that you may encounter with fingerpicking.

Practicing **all the patterns** will not only develop your dexterity in regards to fingerpicking, but it will also get you to start "thinking outside of the box" and coming up with your own patterns. Depending on the genre of music, picking with your nails is preferred over not having nails and playing with your fingertips. Classical, Spanish and flamenco styles almost always require the use of fingernails while country "chicken pickin'" sounds better when you don't have nails.

YOU are the artist here. You get to choose what best suits you. Be open and experiment with some different styles to see what you're most comfortable with.

Fingerpicking Exercises - Songs in 4

<u>1</u>	<u>2</u>	<u>3</u>	<u>4</u>
P	I	M	A
P	I	A	M
P	M	I	A
P	M	A	I
P	A	M	I
P	A	I	M

1	2	3	4
P	M A	P	M A
P	I M	P	I M
P	I A	P	I A
P	M A	P	I M
P	I M	P	M A
P	I M A	P	I M A

1	2	3	4
P A	M	I	M
P I	M	A	M
P M	I	A	I
P M	I	P A	I
P A	I	P M	I
P I	M	I	A

Fingerpicking Exercises - Songs in 6

1	2	3	4	5	6
P	I	M	A	M	I
P	M	I	A	M	I
P	M	A	M	I	M
P	I	A	M	A	M
P	M	A	M	I	M
P	A	M	I	M	I
P	A	I	M	I	M

1	2	3	4	5	6
P	I M A	I M A	P	I M A	I M A
P	I M	I M	P	M A	M A
P	I A	I A	P	I M	I M

Chapter 21:

Discover Uke Scale Maps and How to Successfully Use Them to Play All Your Favorite Uke Tunes

Songs are comprised of melodies and chords. The notes that make up those melodies and chords create a specific "key" or tonal center. The tonal center has notes that "relate" to it better than other notes. For example, the key of C major has the set of notes that follow: C, D, E, F, G, A, B. It's not to say that you cannot go out of this scale, but usually you would not and the notes will sound more cohesive and will seem to "match" better, when in one particular key. Every tonal center has a different set of matching notes. This is also known as a scale.

In the following section I have included some popular scales used in music for 1000s of years. To use this in practice, find a song in a particular key and use that scale map to guide you in the notes that will compliment that song.

Major Scale Maps

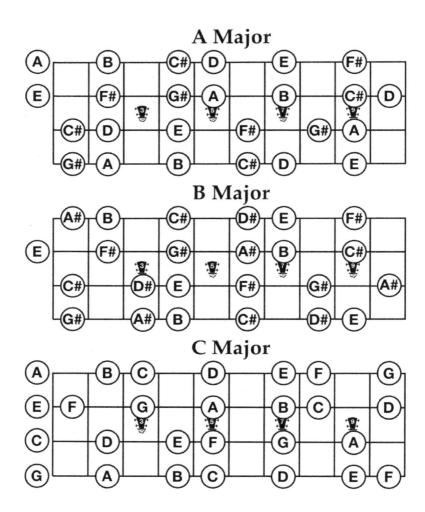

A Major

B Major

C Major

126

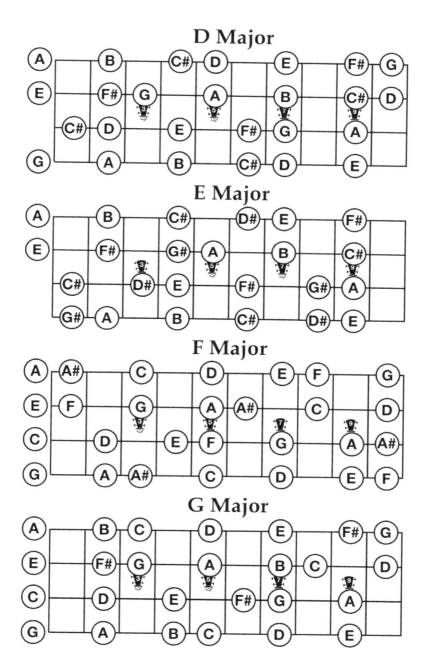

Blues Scale Maps

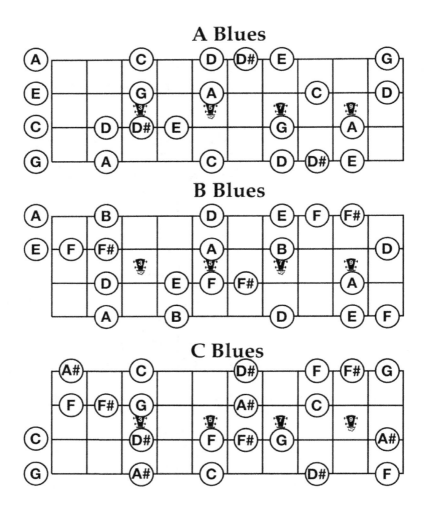

128

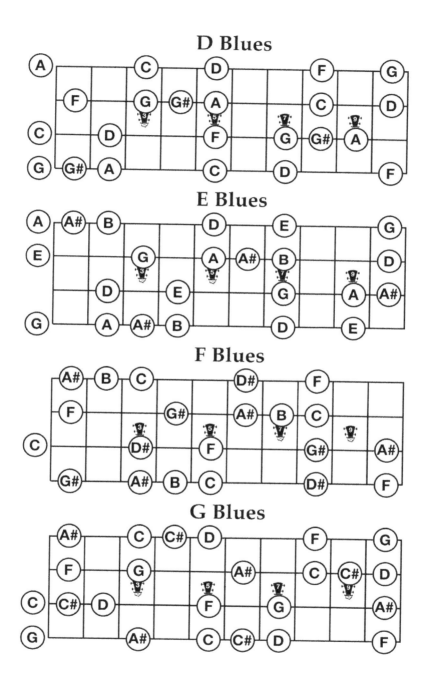

Chapter 22:

How to Read Chord Charts - Song Examples

The following pages are our song examples that I refer to in the chapter, "How to Read Chord Charts". Please read that chapter again while referring to these song charts.

Counting Song

IN 4 CAPO 2 (C feel)

INT:	C G/B	A- F	C G/B	A- F
VRS:	C G/B	A- F	C G/B	A- F
	C D-	A- F	C D-	A- F
CHR:	G	F	G	F
VRS:	C G/B	A- F	C G/B	A- F
	C D-	A- F	C D-	A- F
CHR:	G	F	G	F
VRS:	C G/B	A- F	C G/B	A- F
	C D-	A- F	C D-	A- F

131

12-Bar Blues in A

<u>In 4</u>

A^7	A^7	A^7	A^7
D^7	D^7	A^7	A^7
E^7	D^7	A^7	A^7

Amazing Grace

<u>In 3</u>

G	G	C	G
E-	C	D	D
G	G	C	G
E-	D	G	G

Amazing Grace (Number System)

<u>In 3</u>

1	1	4	1
6-	4	5	5
1	1	4	1
6-	5	1	1

Apple Pie

<u>IN 4 (Key of G)</u>

CHR:			
<u>G C</u>	<u>G D</u>	<u>G C</u>	<u>G D</u>
<u>G C</u>	<u>G D</u>	E-	A^7
E-	D^7	D^7	

VRS:			
G	A-	C	A-
E-	D	D	<u>G D</u>
E-	A-	C	E-
A^7	D^7	D^7	E-
A-	E-	A-	<u>C G</u>
A^7	C	D^7	<u>G D</u>
E-	A-	C	<u>G D</u>
E-	C	C	<u>G C</u>
<u>G D^7</u>			

Big Cheater

IN 4 Capo 2 (G feel)

INT:	E-	D	C	D
	E-	D	C	B7
VRS:	E-	D	C	B7
	E-	D	C	B7
	E-	D	C	B7
	A-	A-	B7	B7
CHR:	C	E-	C	E-
	C	E-	B7	B7
	C	E-	C	E-
	C	B7		
TA:	E-	D	C	B7
VRS:	AGAIN			
CHR:	AGAIN			
BRG:	E-	E-	G	D
	C	C	A-	A-
	B7	B7		
TA:	E-	D	C	B7
	E-	D	C	B7
CHR:	AGAIN			

135

Big Cheater (Number System)

<u>IN 4 Capo 2 (G feel)</u>

<u>INT:</u>	6-	5	4	5
	6-	5	4	3^7
<u>VRS:</u>	6-	5	4	3^7
	6-	5	4	3^7
	6-	5	4	3^7
	2-	2-	3^7	3^7
<u>CHR:</u>	4	6-	4	6-
	4	6-	3^7	3^7
	4	6-	4	6-
	4	3^7		
<u>TA:</u>	6-	5	4	3^7
<u>VRS:</u>	AGAIN			
<u>CHR:</u>	AGAIN			
<u>BRG:</u>	6-	6-	1	5
	4	4	2-	2-
	3^7	3^7		
<u>TA:</u>	6-	5	4	3^7
	6-	5	4	3^7
<u>CHR:</u>	AGAIN			

Ellen

IN 4

INT:	[:C	C	E-	E-:]
VRS:	E-	E-	E-	C
	C E-	E-	E-	E-
	C	C E-		
CHR:	[:E-7	E-6	C/E	E-:]
VRS:	E-	E-	E-	C
	C E-	E-	E-	E-
	C	C E-		
CHR:	[:E-7	E-6	C/E	E-:]
INT:	[:C	C	E-	E-:]
VRS:	E-	E-	E-	C
	C E-	E-	E-	E-
	C	C E-		
CHR:	[:E-7	E-6	C/E	E-:]

Hurry

IN 6 Capo 5 (G feel)

INT:	G	E-	G	E-
VRS:	G	E-	G	E-
	C	D	G	D
	G	C D	E-	C
	D	B-	E-	E-
CHR:	C	C	E-	E-
	C	C	G	D
	G	D		

Verse and chorus 3x total, then

VRS:	G	E-	G	E-
	C	D	G	D
	G	C D	E-	C
	D	B-	E-	E-
CHR4:	C	C	E-	E-
	C	C	G	D
	C	C	E-	E-
	C	C	G	D
	G			

Hurry (Number System)

<u>IN 6 Capo 5 (G feel)</u>

<u>INT</u>:	1	6-	1	6-
<u>VRS</u>:	1	6-	1	6-
	4	5	1	5
	1	<u>4 5</u>	6-	4
	5	3-	6-	6-
<u>CHR</u>:	4	4	6-	6-
	4	4	1	5
	5			

Verse and chorus 2x, then

<u>VRS</u>:	1	6-	1	6-
	4	5	1	5
	1	<u>4 5</u>	6-	4
	5	3-	6-	6-
<u>CHR4</u>:	4	4	6-	6-
	4	4	1	5
	4	4	6-	6-
	4	4	1	5
	1			

Hurts

<u>IN 4 (CAPO 1 G feel)</u>

<u>INT:</u>	[:E-	D	C	C:]
<u>VRS:</u>	E-	D	C	C
	E-	D	C	C
	C	<u>C D</u>	E-	<u>E- D</u>
	C	C	C	D
<u>CHR:</u>	E-	<u>E- D</u>	C	C
	G	G	D	D
	E-	<u>E- D</u>	C	C
	G	G	DSUS	D
<u>TA:</u>	E-	D	C	C

Verse and chorus again, then
     ||| P

<u>BRG:</u>	<u>C D</u>	D	C	
<u>SOLO:</u>	E-	<u>E- D</u>	C	<u>C D</u>
	E-	D	C	
<u>CHR:</u>	E-	<u>E- D</u>	C	C
	G	G	D	D
	E-	<u>E- D</u>	C	C
	G	G	DSUS	D
	C	C	DSUS	D

Summary

WOW, you made it!!! Not just through this book, but through understanding some of the most important subjects in regards to the ukulele. I have been playing for nearly 30 years and know MANY uke players that have been playing that long that don't know many of these concepts. SOO, it really is a big deal that you have made it this far.

All of these concepts, ideas, definitions and exercises were designed to give you more "colors" in your palette. <u>YOU</u> are the artist! Don't let anything that you have learned here or from anywhere else hinder your art. It's NOT about rules! However, all these bits and pieces are going to help you decipher the code of music. They will allow you to play new parts that you would not have thought of before, had you not stretched your mind.

Everyone has different goals and different skills that they bring to the table, including YOU. Don't be discouraged about what another can do "better" than you. You have your own skills and goals. You are unique! I can't express that enough! EVERYONE has a place in the musical spectrum. SOO, practice and use what you are going to use for YOUR goals and forget the rest. You can always come back to it and refresh your memory. Having taken the time to go through the whole regimen however will allow you to KNOW what you need and what you don't. Plus, it will just make you a better musician overall.

I'm proud of you! I want to hear from you and about your accomplishments on this beautiful and exciting instrument called the ukulele. Send me pics, send me stories, and let your friends know of the lessons. I plan on teaching 50 years from now, so I'm not going anywhere. Stick with me and I'll stick with you!

And remember the final and most IMPORTANT of all the lessons: Practice, practice, practice!!

Thank You

Before you go I would like to say a big "thank you" for purchasing and reading my book. I know you could have easily purchased someone else's book on ukulele lessons and how to play the uke. But you took a chance with mine. Huge thanks for buying and finishing it.

If you liked this book then I need your help real quick!

Please take a few moments to leave a review for this book on Amazon.

Your feedback with continue to help me provide you and everyone else with more uke books. And if you really liked it then please let me know :)

One Last Thing My Friend...

If you feel like other people could benefit from the material that is in this book then feel free to share it with your friends.

Thanks again!

http://www.facebook.com/yourguitarsage
http://www.twitter.com/yourguitarsage

A Cause Close to My Heart

As many of you know, I am a BIG animal lover and advocate for animal welfare. I also believe to be of great significance in this world, we need to leave more than we have taken and we MUST take a stand for those that don't have a voice.

Two things that I have always been passionate about are music and animals. If you have a heart for animals like I do, you will be happy to know that a portion of every book purchase is given to animal welfare organizations like:

www.TribeOfHeart.org and
www.HappyTalesHumane.com

Many people have not taken the time to understand the gravity or plight of many of the animals living in our world today. Since the cause is so big, I have focused my cause on the issues of "spay and neuter" and animal cruelty prevention through legislation, law enforcements and education. "Spay and neuter" is also known as animal population control or the sterilization of domesticated (house) pets and feral (wild) animals where necessary and able.

It's a simple procedure that can save millions of animals' lives every year from the carelessness/cruelty. Here are some basic facts to show you just how quickly one cat or dog left to breed can have a DRASTIC impact on the death toll.

Cat		Dog	
1st year	3 liters = 12 offspring	1st year	4 offspring with 2 females
2nd year	144 offspring	2nd year	12 offspring
3rd year	1,728 offspring	3rd year	36 offspring
4th year	10,736 offspring	4th year	324 offspring

If you are a pet owner, I IMPLORE you to spay/neuter your animal. This is an EASY way to change 1000s of innocent lives. Oh yeah, and what comes around goes around. Blessings come from such acts.

Also, if you feel moved to do so, please give to the organizations above. Together, we have the power to change this world! *Please join me!*

Resources

**Lesson #1
(Anatomy of the Uke, left and right
technique, beginner exercises,
encouragement and advice)**

www.yourguitarsage.com/lesson-one-uke

**Lesson #2
(How to think about the ukulele as a
guitar player, basic music theory, notes on
the uke)**

www.yourguitarsage.com/lesson-two-uke

Tuning Your Uke by Ear

www.yourguitarsage.com/tune-by-ear-ukulele

Strumming method

www.yourguitarsage.com/strumming-lesson-uke

How to Read Charts

www.yourguitarsage.com/chord-charts-ukulele

How to Play Bar Chords

www.yourguitarsage.com/bar-chords-ukulele

#1 *Amazon.com* Bestseller *Guitar Mastery Simplified*

Guitar Mastery Simplified: How Anyone Can Quickly Become a Strumming, Chords and Lead Guitar Ninja

www.GuitarMasterySimplified.com

#1 *Amazon.com* Bestseller *How to Read Music*

www.HowToReadMusicBook.com

Here's Your 25 Free Guitar Videos – MUST WATCH For All Guitar Players

www.GettingStartedPlayingGuitar.com

Your Guitar Sage Main Website

www.YourGuitarSage.com

How to Master Your Right and Left Hand Techniques – Free Video Course

www.UnstoppableGuitarSystem.com

Your Guitar Sage Videos

www.youtube.com/yourguitarsage

Your Uke Sage

www.yourukesage.com

YouTube/yourukesage

www.youtube.com/yourukesage

Intro to Your Uke Sage

www.yourguitarsage.com/intro-uke-sage

Made in the USA
Las Vegas, NV
09 February 2021